AF073538

On Holiday

Level 7 – Turquoise

Helpful Hints for Reading at Home

The graphemes (written letters) and phonemes (units of sound) used throughout this series are aligned with Letters and Sounds. This offers a consistent approach to learning whether reading at home or in the classroom.

HERE IS A LIST OF PHONEMES FOR THIS PHASE OF LEARNING. AN EXAMPLE OF THE PRONUNCIATION CAN BE FOUND IN BRACKETS.

Phase 5			
ay (day)	ou (out)	ie (tie)	ea (eat)
oy (boy)	ir (girl)	ue (blue)	aw (saw)
wh (when)	ph (photo)	ew (new)	oe (toe)
au (Paul)	a_e (make)	e_e (these)	i_e (like)
o_e (home)	u_e (rule, cube)		

Phase 5 Alternative Pronunciations of Graphemes			
a (hat, what)	e (bed, she)	i (fin, find)	o (hot, so, other)
u (but, unit)	c (cat, cent)	g (got, giant)	ow (cow, blow)
ie (tied, field)	ea (eat, bread)	er (farmer, herb)	ch (chin, school, chef)
y (yes, by, very)	ou (out, shoulder, could, you)		

HERE ARE SOME WORDS WHICH YOUR CHILD MAY FIND TRICKY.

Phase 5 Tricky Words			
oh	their	people	Mr
Mrs	looked	called	asked
could			

TOP TIPS FOR HELPING YOUR CHILD TO READ:

- Allow children time to break down unfamiliar words into units of sound and then encourage children to string these sounds together to create the word.
- Encourage your child to point out any focus phonics when they are used.
- Read through the book more than once to grow confidence.
- Ask simple questions about the text to assess understanding.
- Encourage children to use illustrations as prompts.

This book focuses on the alternative pronunciation of the grapheme /o/ and is a Turquoise level 7 book band.

Can you sort these words into two groups?
One group has o as in **fold**.
One group has o as in **hot**.

bolt

not

crop

cold

stop

block

molt

Have you ever been on holiday? We will go on holiday in this book. We can go to lots of different parts of the planet!

People get around the planet on planes. The pilot sits in the front of the plane. It is called the cockpit. It has lots of controls.

It is hot in Morocco. You can feel the heat when the plane door opens. In Morocco, you can go onto the beach and into the sea.

Morocco

You can go to markets in Morocco. You can meet local sellers who will sell you gifts for money. You might get a shirt or a toy.

It is time to go onto the next part of the planet! In Brazil, you can find the Amazon rainforest and the Amazon River. You can see lots of animals.

You can see monkeys in the trees. They swing from tree to tree. You can see dolphins in the Amazon River too. They have a pink shade.

Now we can go to a cold part of the planet. Put on a scarf and a coat if you go to Finland.

Forest in Finland

In Finland, you might go in a hot sauna to get out of the cold. Finland has a lot of good spots for a photo.

Onto another cold part of the planet! People go to the Alps to ski. They ski down the hills. Could you ski like a pro?

Lots of people also stay in a log cabin among the hills. A log cabin can be a home for when you are away.

You do not have to travel far to go on holiday. It can be a lot of fun to stay near to home.

Pack up the car!

I wonder which part of the planet you will go to. Whether it is hot or cold, have the best time ever on holiday!

©2022 **BookLife Publishing Ltd.**
King's Lynn, Norfolk, PE30 4LS, UK

ISBN 978-1-80155-812-9

All rights reserved. Printed in Poland.
A catalogue record for this book is available from the British Library.

On Holiday
Written by William Anthony
Designed by Drue Rintoul

An Introduction to BookLife Readers...

Our Readers have been specifically created in line with the London Institute of Education's approach to book banding and are phonetically decodable and ordered to support each phase of the Letters and Sounds document.

Each book has been created to provide the best possible reading and learning experience. Our aim is to share our love of books with children, providing both emerging readers and prolific page-turners with beautiful books that are guaranteed to provoke interest and learning, regardless of ability.

BOOK BAND GRADED using the Institute of Education's approach to levelling.

PHONETICALLY DECODABLE supporting each phase of Letters and Sounds.

EXERCISES AND QUESTIONS to offer reinforcement and to ascertain comprehension.

CLEAR DESIGN to inspire and provoke engagement, providing the reader with clear visual representations of each non-fiction topic.

AUTHOR INSIGHT:
WILLIAM ANTHONY

William Anthony's involvement with children's education is quite extensive. He has written over 60 titles with BookLife Publishing so far, across a wide range of subjects. William graduated from Cardiff University with a 1st Class BA (Hons) in Journalism, Media and Culture, creating an app and a TV series, among other things, during his time there.

William Anthony has also produced work for the Prince's Trust, a charity created by HRH The Prince of Wales, that helps young people with their professional future. He has created animated videos for a children's education company that works closely with the charity.

This book focuses on the alternative pronunciation of the grapheme /o/ and is a turquoise level 7 book band.

Image Credits Images are courtesy of Shutterstock.com. With thanks to Getty Images, Thinkstock Photo and iStockphoto. Cover – GOLFX, Iakov Kalinin, ayelet-keshet. p4–5 – Niyazz, Angelo Giampiccolo. p6–7 – Ana Flasker, cktravels.com. p8–9 – Wirestock Creators, Dirk M. de Boer, COULANGES. p10–11 – BlueOrange Studio, Wasim Khuzam. p12–13 – gorillaimages, FooTToo. p14–15 – Odua Images, Monkey Business Images.